The fact that you hav_____ __ __p this book means that you have an interest in Guinea Pigs. For my brother Peter, they became his life, and the expertise that he acquired regarding their care has been well documented in his previous books. Those of you who knew him will be familiar with his ramblings about the veterinary profession, royalty, and both central and local government. His books have also hinted at other things he loved in life – his jazz, his ladies, the age of steam and the Bedfordshire countryside. Peter's fight with cancer was a long one but one battle he was not to win, and in the last few months of his life he made careful plans to ensure his guinea pigs went to good homes through the many friends he had made and who had supported him during his illness.

He spoke of this book, which he had been working on for some time, in which he gave his guinea pigs the chance to give their view of what life was like living with Peter Gurney. Whilst it may not add a great deal to the base of knowledge about guinea pigs, it does reflect his particular humour and captures his skills with a camera. Peter's death on July 1st 2006 brought tributes from around the world, and those folk I met at this time encouraged me to publish this small tribute to my brother, who could perhaps be described as **the last of their kind** or, as he would have put it **"Himself"**.

Doug Gurney

October 2006

Other Books by Peter Gurney

Title	Publisher
The Proper Care of Guinea Pigs	TFH
Piggy Potions	TFH
What's My Guinea Pig	TFH
The Sex Life of Guinea Pigs	TFH
Guinea Pig Family Pet Guide	Collins
All of Their Kind	Peter Gurney
More of Their Kind	Peter Gurney

Peter Gurney © Copyright 2006

All rights reserved

No parts of this publication may be reproduced, stored in a retrieval system, or transmitted in any form or by any means, electronic, mechanical, photocopying, recording or otherwise without the prior permission of the copyright owner.

British Library Cataloguing In Publication Data
A Record of this Publication is available
from the British Library

ISBN 978-1-84685-657-0

First Published 2007 by
Exposure Publishing,
an imprint of
Diggory Press Ltd
Three Rivers, Minions, Liskeard, Cornwall, PL14 5LE, UK
and of Diggory Press, Inc.,
Goodyear, Arizona, USA
WWW.DIGGORYPRESS.COM

Preface

We have been observing 'Himself' for quite a few years now, indeed we have written about him on his website in the 'View From The Pen' section. 'Himself' is none other than our obedient servant who writes the books about us.

Very early on in his relationship with our kind, we put him right about his position in the scheme of things. We didn't have to lecture him, just let him learn how it was, by the services he was expected to provide for the honour of having us live with him. These are: providing luxurious housing, fresh green and dry feed daily, an adequate water supply, and comprehensive cleaning services.

On the personal front, we demand top rate veterinary care and husbandry, which can include everything from syringe feeding us when we are sick and cannot feed ourselves, to cleaning our backsides when we get the squits or the male members suffer from anal impaction when they get old!
We expect, and now get, access to a brilliant veterinary surgeon when our health problems are beyond his expertise and full nursing care.

What does he get in return? ---------US! Nuff said!

The pictures in this book show us in all our glory and prove, beyond a shadow of doubt, that we are the most magnificent creatures on this planet. We have style, elegance, and grace and enhance the world and all that is in it by our charm, cuteness, good looks and above all, our humble demeanour!

In the extracts from 'View From The Pen' it will be made abundantly clear that we are also extremely tolerant wee beasties, particularly with our particular servant, whose strange ways we have learned to live with. In the main, we try and ignore him when he is doing his own thing, which is seldom a pretty sight and always an odd one. If he is a good sample of human kind, then we can only ponder on what went wrong at the design stage!

The Management

Chapter One

A Queenly Cavy

Sarah

Some of us just have it, poise, and a power of command over beings lesser than we are! Sarah, a Peruvian, is a pretty good example of this and we had no end of trouble when she first arrived. There was much gnashing of teeth, raised hackles and 'do you think you're hard enough?' expressions from her if any of us so much as looked at her. As for Himself, she made it clear, right from the start that she would be picked up and petted only when she wanted to and not when he felt the need, except if it coincided with her desires at that particular time.

Needless to say, the more she plays hard to get with him, the more he panders to her desires; calls her an Alpha pig, rather than a right bitch, which she can still be.

She has him right under her paws. When she puts on her snuggle bunny act; he goes 'Ahh', and her wish will be his command! Even allowing for the fact that we are all well aware that we are the superior species, Himself really is pathetically smitten with this Madam.

When she was a mum, he really did lose the plot completely and anyone would have thought that he had fathered them, the way he strutted about the place, Peacock proud and expecting his friends to fall to their knees and worship at the altar of her motherhood!

View From The Pen
It Was All Happening

We ask you! There he was, on his hands and knees, naked as the day he was born, with a camera in hand at one thirty in the morning. Yes, we know that you don't really want to go there but we had to so why shouldn't you lot!

Bitsy had decided that it was time to litter down and he was awakened by the sounds of her first contractions as the first one was about to come into this breathing world. He had put his camera in the box instead of leaving it handy on the shelf as he usually does when one of us is about to litter down. A boy scout he aint!

He is not at his best at that time in the morning, so was all fingers and thumbs, trying to flick open the catches of the box in his haste to get the shots. His knickers were in a tight knot by the time he had sorted himself out, so the language was appalling but we are all well used to that, for we are frequently subjected to it whenever he throws his rattle out of his pram.

By the time he took up his position, the second baby was out and the third well on it's way. We, of course, all deliberately got in the way in order to mess up his shots. We are not the stupid bitches that he called us, we simply know where his keyhole is and enjoy inserting our keys and winding him up. Hee- hee- hee!

We gave him a break in the end and let him get a few shots of the action but managed to mess up the best ones. You should have heard it all, it sounded like a top fashion shoot. 'That's it, that's it!' he yelled, 'Hold it. Hold it!' As if, Bitsy would pause mid-contraction, face the camera and say cheese!

The man's a total airhead, and we are pleased to report that Bitsy would immediately speed up her action whenever she was urged to slow it down. In the event, the babe shot out like a pea from a pod so himself didn't get the longed for halfway-out shot! You would really think that he would know better by now - we do not perform on cue, or if we do, it will be to do the very opposite of what he requires us to do. Being contrary is a very important part of our job description!

Himself now, after the event? Well, he has got over his attack of the vapours but he is a mere human being, and a male one at that, so it will be a few weeks before he really gets over the excitement for what we all regard as the rather mundane business of giving birth!

Chapter Two
Kingly Cavy

Iggy

Iggy, a Crested, has been with us for three years now and he is class from the tip of his nose to his curvaceous cob shaped butt, which is generous but in proportion to his size and weight.

As he is free range, he can stand up against the glass front of our pen and poke his nose over the top whenever he feels so inclined. However, unlike many of the other free range males that have roamed outside, rumble strutting, he is always dignified and has never been known to make crude remarks about us ourselves.

We wish that his free range mate, Jake, behaved with the same decorum. He not only makes very crude suggestions and invites us to try him, free of charge; he hooks his forepaws over the glass front of our pen and twitches his hips in a most suggestive manner! However, he is young and it is hoped that he will acquire manners and proper respectfulness with age.

Iggy and Jake

Whenever Himself hauls out his camera bag to do an outdoor shoot, he invariably takes Iggy along with him and one of us girls. Not only is he a good poser, content to stand or sit to command, he will lift his head, give full face, profile or whatever, and when the lady who has gone out on the shoot with him is placed alongside him to get a double shot, he will not immediately try and mount her - it isn't going to be that kind of book!

But Of Course We Are!

View From The Pen
The Man is Mad

There is no doubt about it, Himself is mad. He has been having one of his funny periods during which he dunks us all and sticks needles in us. He said it was because there had been some kind of bugs in our pen. OK, then why doesn't he dunk the bugs and stick needles in them? Even the nice lady vet, whom we thought was on our side, supplied the necessary medicine and shampoo for him to inflict this terrible treatment.

If that wasn't enough to put us through, his friend in San Diego sent him some more tapes of jazz, so we have had both our ears and our eyes subjected to that. Our eyes? Well, he has this nasty habit of putting these tapes on when he has a bath and unlike any respectable human animal, he seldom dries himself and puts on his bathrobe in the bathroom, which means he comes back into the living room and dances and cavorts about, and this is even before he has had any of that amber liquid. We could understand this if he was out of his skull, but I ask you, sober and fresh from the bath?!

It is not a very pleasant sight for ladies of our refinement, particularly when it occurs around carrot time, which it often does. Just think of it from our point of view and our line of sight. No, we won't draw you a picture, you may be eating while you are reading this, and why should we inflict what we have to go through, in such detail, upon our readers.

Even Olga de Polga, who was staying with us last week, remarked upon it and assured us that this kind of thing never happens in the Bond household. So it looks as though this kind of behaviour could be unique to our own human. I wonder if we could get him to have some therapy for this problem he has of thinking that displaying his bits and pieces to innocent ladies like us is at all enjoyable. What he has to display, we can firmly state, is not in the slightest bit impressive.

We have all come to the conclusion that living with human beings can be kind of an equivocal experience. It's nice not to have to go out and forage for our food, but not nice to see the human in the raw, so to speak. It's nice not to have to bother about the weather outside but a bit of a bind having to hear the funny sounds they make and listen to.

Chapter Three
Out and About

We get to go out with Himself now and again to see the sights when he goes on a photo-shoot. We get hauled around in a trailer that's fixed to the back of his bike. It can be a bit noisy and bumpy but he always ensures that there are lots of goodies to nibble on between shoots, so we don't complain too much.

Needless to say, as many of these photo shoots are in the kind of places where there are lots of human tourists, we always attract lots of admirers, many of whom have guinea pigs themselves. The latter are obviously those that are far further advanced down the evolutionary scale in the human species!

What follows in this chapter are pictures of us strutting our stuff, out-posing any of those human models you would see on a fashion catwalk, and, in our case we design our own clothes and attend to our own grooming, Enjoy!

Muffy and Obliging Friend

Manda and Bridie

'Come on, let's knock on the door. The flag's there so she must be in.'

Flossy

'As I was saying in the House only yesterday…...'

Garreth and Giggles.

'Comfortable?'

Bridie and Sarah

'Hm......, London Eye? It looks like a Ferris - Wheel to me!'

Ruby

'Roll up, roll up, all aboard for the Skylark!'

At the Admiralty

'Well, …… hello sailor!

Big Ben and Little Daisy

Morgan

Doing The Tour - Richmond Bridge

Giggles and Gareth

View From The Pen
They'll Be Some Changes Made

We all reckon that Himself is going through the male menopause, late in life. We have had yet another change to this place. He has bought himself a bunk bed. There is a bunk bed at the top and a futon at the bottom, which acts like a sofa and can be converted into a double bed when required. Perhaps we had better draw a veil of the 'When required' bit. We won't go there, eh!

He shut the free rangers, Jake and Jasper, into the kitchen when he began putting it all together. It was the best place for them for he can be ham-fisted and would probably have stood on them or dropped a hammer on their heads. The language was somewhat ripe during the construction work but as he was probably reading the instructions upside down and was in a rush to get the thing up, this was not at all surprising.

Well, after he had finally managed to put it all together, he let the boys back in. They both rushed in, obviously not pleased at being shut up in the kitchen for a couple of hours, kind of skidded to a halt and threw into reverse gear, PDQ. Typical males, anything new and their bottle goes. However, even we girls got a bit of a fright the following morning when his voice came from way up above our heads yet he was out of sight on the bunk. For a brief second, we thought it was God on high, but as he began to climb down the ladder we saw that it was only a too-mortal being. The sight of his bare backside descending the ladder is not the kind of thing you want to see when you are just about to get tucked into your breakfast. Now, when we know he is about to get up, we all turn our backs and look at the wall until he is down on the floor and has put his knickers on.

We have got used to the idea that every so often he will change things; it's something to do with his genes perhaps, or the aging of them. One thing is for sure, there is no way that he will change now; he is far too long in the tooth and fixed in his ways. Did you know that in March this year he will start picking up his retirement pension? Now that, when ranked along side our life spans, is really ancient. He reckons he still feels like an eighteen year old - but he acts more like a six year old for most of the time. Pity he doesn't look like one, particularly each morning when he reverses down that ladder!

Chapter Four
Fun Time

We don't have toys to play with in our pens because we are far too busy eating and sleeping but when we get let loose in a photographic studio, we can boogie on down like the best of them. Of course, we enjoy winding him up sometimes by turning our backs and showing him a nice broad butt and not the cute face he was expecting just as he hits that shutter button, but in the main we co-operate, for we reckon it's good PR for the species.

'Hi, I'm Olly or Owl Face as they call me…..'

'…..and I'm Gerty, and they call me Gorgeous!'

Piratical Piggies

'Hey, where's the driver gone?'

Four Of A Kind…..

……. beats three aces!

'I don't go anywhere without my teddy.'

'Are you sure this thing's safe…..?'

'Tis if your mum uses her head!'

'Grab your coat, Babe,…. you've pulled!'

Can't play, but a great little mover!

'Hmm…., must get a pair of glasses.'

'I did do well!'

'What's Piggy Hot Pot, boss?'

'I am not at all sure about this!'

'Doh, Ray, Me, Far…..

…..Far, Me, Ray, Doh!'

'Hey big boy….. cut it out!'

'Are they still there?'

'Oh! shut your face, I'm pushing as hard as I can.'

'I've finished mum, can you come and wipe my bum?'

'Oh no, not the school run again!'

Beware the Woodland Wobbly Pig

Koji, the Woodland Wonder Pig

Dish of The Day

'Don't throw us out!'

'I'm Daisy…. Fly Me!'

'I'm George....I ain't going no where!'

View From The Pen

Big heads!

Oh dear! there was nothing we could do with them, Himself and Blazer, after they had come back from a book signing session at the Doncaster Show. We all knew that it would be like that but hey, what else did we expect - they are both male and like all of their kind, they need their egos massaged now and again or they go into a decline. We sows know that we are the superior sex, so we don't need it. We simply looked on, tolerantly, as they preened themselves after their brief afternoon of fame.

Himself was delighted because many of the nice young ladies kept telling him how wonderful he was and they insisted that they have their photographs taken with him. Blazer loved it because the self same females kept saying that they wanted to take him home with them, and fed and snogged him a lot.

We didn't let on that we all thought that they were silly little boys, well most of us didn't. However, there was one of us who brought him back down to earth, and that was Ruby.

Later in the evening, while he was sipping from a glass of that Amber liquid that makes him grin a lot and jig about to his Jazz CDs, he scooped Ruby up and plonked her down on his lap. The jazz continued and it was clear that he was feeling very smug and pleased with himself. Then, without prior warning, he suddenly felt a warm wet feeling, spreading over his thighs. Ruby had expressed all our scorn by peeing on him. Serves him right for feeding her half a damned cucumber while we sat looking on, salivating!

After he put Ruby back in the pen, we all gave her a round of applause and greeted her with 'Well done, kid!'. Hmm ...... praised by his own kind in the afternoon, peed on by our kind in the evening - that evened things up a bit! How were the mighty fallen!

Chapter Five
Mums

To say that we are good at being mums is as superfluous as saying that the sun rises each morning. We usually set the whole business into motion at about five months of age, and then, unlike the human species, when about two and a half months later we tackle the mechanics of producing our young, there is no more fuss about it than as if we were simply settling down to eat our breakfast.

Not for us the pre natal exercises, or programmed monitoring by doctors and nurses, and certainly no written instructions in a book on how it should be done. We treat it like sex, a natural function - when the feeling's upon you.... go for it girls!

We only wish Himself was less of a hypocrite about it all. Time and time again we have heard him on the phone, reassuring people whose guinea pigs were getting near to littering down, that all was well and it was all perfectly normal and there was nothing to concern themselves over. However, when any of us are a few days over the date he thinks that we are due, there he is, biting his nails, and the longer we linger, the more he gets his knickers in a knot. It's great fun, and we try to hang it out for as long as we can.

Plenty milk…..

…..plenty grow….

…..plenty play!

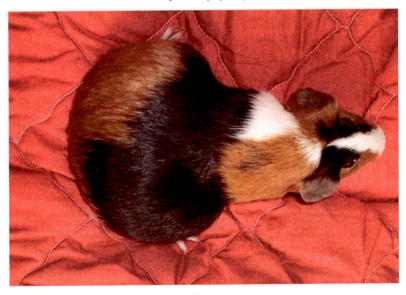

Cooking!

'That's two, one to go.'

'That's it, number three, a full set'.

'Smile for the camera.'

'Me next, me next!'

'Only the one, but ain't she precious….

…..and look how she grew…..

……into a glorious fluff ball, named Fifi.'

View From The Pen
Wee ones

Emma did her stuff a few days ago, a week earlier than Himself expected her to. She littered down and had three babies. One unfortunately didn't make it but the other two were fine. They are two lovely girls and have been named Rosemary and Kate. Rosemary is the quiet one, and Kate the noisy one who has had a lot to say for herself ever since the day she was born.

We all lend a hand baby-sitting when mum goes away into a quiet corner for a rest. We groom them and let them snuggle up to us on the rare occasions when they get tired, after pop corning all over the pen. Himself was hoping for at least one boy that he could put in with his daddy, Mr Bumble, and he had a very long face for a couple of days when the boy died.

Emma and the girls have already been up to the Children's Hospital where they were all much admired. The nurses kept picking up the babies, putting them in their tunic pockets and going off to show their friends. Those nurses are obviously ladies of great good taste, knowing a real piece of class when they see it - guinea pig flesh!

Himself has informed us that these particular babies will be staying with us so we can watch them growing up to be great big beautiful babes like we are. He thinks they are going to be big girls and so do we, and so they should be, from the amount of suckling they get from Emma. And hey, they were both into their dry feed and eating grass when they were only two days old. We don't mean the odd nibble here and there, like you see in most babies, this was full-hearted munching, so they are getting a really good start in life.

Needless to say, we have lots of visitors coming to admire these new additions, which of course make Himself show off like mad. Never mind, we guess his fixation with these and us all keeps him off street corners and getting into all sorts of trouble.

Chapter Six
At Home

We are rather comfortable here, nice large quarters, bedding changed regularly and a plentiful supply of food and water. The drawback is Himself. All guineas need a Himself or Herself to cater for their needs when they are domesticated. They are usually noisy and if they are all like ours, spend a great deal of time gawping at us. Ours also likes to take lots of photographs of us, and though we are all, of course, very photogenic it does get a bit tiresome being sneaked up on and surprised by a damn great flash.

Perhaps our man is unique and it is just our bad luck to have been landed with him. However, we refuse to be phased by him so we carry on regardless, getting our revenge by peeing and pooping on him when he is settled down with one of us on his lap.

Butterscotch. 'Hmm…., not as good as the 88, but quite a fine bouquet.'

Gavin, being Cucumber Cute!

'You looking at me?'

Daisy at the Water Hole

'What's in there, dad?'
'Females…… You're too young!'

The Girls at the Bar

'Oh dear…..I shouldn't have had that last beer!'

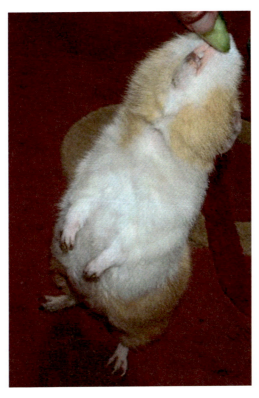

A Performing Seal Guinea Pig!

My Boy!!!!!

'Hey, did you hear about her at Number Eight - disgusting!'

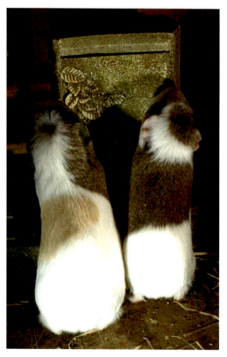

Gert and Daisy…… Girls Night Out!

View From The Pen
It's Hol's time

We are more crowded at this time of the year for it is when the humans go on their summer holidays, which means their guineas have to come and board with us. We don't mind, of course, for most of them are old friends. Some were even born here and some of their mums still live here.

Emma, who has been away for a few weeks, sharing a pen with a certain Mr Bumble, a very handsome Peruvian lad with coat markings like a bumble bee, has returned. We are pleased to announce that as a result of her stay with the lad, we are expecting a happy event in a few weeks time. She is eating and drinking for England and is well bulked out in the sides. It seems ages since we have had baby guinea pigs running around in this pen and we are all looking forward to it. Some of us are even thinking of taking up knitting little booties!

Himself, as usual, is hoping that Emma will litter down when he is here so that he can take photographs of her in action, so to speak. Also, as usual, we have told her to wait till he is asleep, and try not to grunt too loud when she has her first contractions or she'll wake him up and out will come the camera.

We have all coped very well with the recent hot weather; with plenty of fans and all the windows open so that we have a nice through draught. Himself was flagging a bit and wilting at the edges; poor old lad isn't built for heat, he prefers the cold weather. Odd bod, really, but comes in handy when it comes to supplying our needs so we'll probably hang onto him. We have often thought of getting a new one but it's all the time and effort it would take to train him or her. You see, they are not very bright in the brain department and you have to scream at them to get them to respond properly, or look cute. It's an age old problem - you can't get the staff these days!

His American friend is coming over in the autumn. She is a female of the species, so consequently is far brighter and happens to think that we are all very snog-worthy. Each morning she gives us what she calls Cavy Candy in the shape of little portions of banana, which she feeds to us individually by hand with lots of nice sweet talk. You see, respect, and a decent kind of service, a lady who knows how to treat ladies! All we get from him is a load of grass or whatever is dish of the day, just bunged in on top of us and a curt, 'Come and get it, girls!'

Way out

Well, that's about it. We would like to thank our sponsors, which are the many visitors who come to admire us, our vet who thinks that we are more than just special - extraordinary is the word she would use - Himself's daughters for supplying the props, and on behalf of Himself we would like to thank us, for being so very tolerant of him!

Ruby, the author!

Lastly, a few of the ramblings Himself wrote about us.

Friend for Life

I'm not a cosy pussy cat or hamster in a cage,
Nor a proud Alsatian dog - for that is far too big.
I'm a kind of snuggle-bug, loved by kids of any age.
A cutie, cobbed shaped cavy kind, they call a Guinea Pig.

Try me, and I think you'll find I'm really rather nice.
I can charm and I can calm and make of you, a friend.
But be warned that I'm for ever, not for once or twice,
For you will fall, they always do, and love me to the end.

Talking to a Friend

Are you there?
As I cut the grass for those who still delight me.
Can you hear me? As I talk to you in my mind,
and sometimes out loud,
Alarming passers-by. I think,
I hope that maybe you might be,
And perhaps, scurry at my feet,
as you did when you were allowed.

If those of my kind could hear me,
knew just to whom I spoke,
They would hurry on,

for fear of other strange things I might do!
For, converse with a Guinea Pig,
a dead one at that, is no joke.
It isn't done.... Not quite the form....
But they didn't know you!

Let them pass by and leave us
to the tenuous link of my longing heart.
Had they known how I felt for you,
would they, could they understand?
I doubt it. "It was only a guinea pig",
they would say, for a start.
"Buy another", they would add,
dismissing you, out of hand.

Poor people, not knowing how we were,
elegant animal and mere man.
For far too short a time you enhanced my life,
then left me to mourn,
And puzzle, Why you? Why me? Why us?
And Why it all wonderfully began?
When my heart would never be my own again,
that day that you were born.

To my elegant, adorable, Chipper

Not You're Average Pig!

I'm not your average guinea pig, I'm Findlay, jack the lad.
I like to make a lot of noise when people are about.
Though I can be a naughty boy, I'm really not too bad,
It's just that when I like to run I also like to shout.

My mate, he's so much quieter and calls me 'Mouth on Legs',
He says "Shut up, you chatter-box, I'm trying to get some kip".
But though I really try my best and do just what he begs,
Once my motor's on the move I have to let it rip.

My mum said that I need a gag to give their ears a rest,
But ear plugs for them all to use would simply do the trick.
Though they call me lots of names like 'Mighty Mouth' and 'Pest',
If they had to choose again, I know it's me they'd pick!

The Goodie Lady

The Goodie Lady's due today, we always know when she's due,
For Standy always grins a lot when she is coming round.
We're practising to salivate, well *you* would, wouldn't you,
Knowing she'll be bringing bags where tummy treats are found!

The Goodie Lady comes today, she's such a change from him.
She doesn't nag or call us bums but smiles and says we're sweet.
Where she is soft and very bright, he's hard and rather dim,
And he is rude and quite a scruff while she is nice and neat!

The Goodie Lady comes today, so shout 'Hip, Hip, Hooray'.
Hang out the flags, bring in the bags, it's munching time again.
We always lighten up our steps on Aunty Sarah's day,
But by the night they're heavier, from all that weight we gain!

Me Bruvver's Gone!

I wonder where me bruvver's gone - I've not seen him for days.
He didn't say that he had plans to leave me on my own.
And though I wouldn't tell him this, I miss his funny ways
And kind of worry he can't cope if he is far from home.

You see we've been a pair so long that both our ways were set,
And though I have a new mate now, a young and spritely lad,
He's not the same as Brother Den, all luscious coat and coronet.
So I miss Denny very much, though he was wild and slightly mad.

He used to tease that long-eared thing, a giant called a 'Rabbit'.
He'd nut it one as he walked by, to make it know it's place,
Or threaten it and nick it's food and do the macho stuff at it.
And sometimes he'd creep up on it and pull a funny face.

And though yon rabbit didn't care and never threatened back,
There is no way that I would try and do what Dennis had.
You see I'm neither brave nor mad, but there's one thing I lack,
It's his cool air of savoir faire which made him such a lad.
I think the Standy misses him even just as much as me.

For he's been hugging me a lot and sometimes looks so sad.
If he has gone where I suspect, then perhaps at last he'll see,
Mr Chipper, Free Range Fred, and many more of us he's had!

To Dusty and Dennis – Are you still begging, 'Pretty Please'?

Barrow Boys

Have you found him Dusty, lad, is he still great fun?
Do you talk of times you had, when you were here with me?
I bet he still creeps up on you and tries to give you one.
I'm sure you let him have his way and sit there patiently,

Tell him that I miss him so, as much as I miss you.
You complimented me each day by making this your home.
I still remember all the warm and funny things you'd do.
The wisest thing I ever did was letting you both roam.

Do you recall the barrow, down at Goodie Lady's place?
When we all went and spent the day and made her laugh a lot.
I know, like me, she misses you, your charm, your cheek and grace.
In both our hearts you'll always have a very special spot.

To my darling boys, Dusty and Dennis.
If there is something after this life,
it's you and **so many of your kind** *that I shall first say "Hi" to.*